CW00537236

pia

Spire Books Ltd
PO Box 2336, Reading RG4 5WI

LD 4729032 3

St Michael and All Angels'
Church, Bedford Park

Contents

This volume is published with the help of a grant from the late Miss Isobel Thornley's Bequest to the University of London.

Spire Books Ltd
PO Box 2336, Reading RG4 5WJ
www.spirebooks.com

CIP data: a catalogue record for this book is available from the British Library
Designed by John Elliott
ISBN 978-1-904965-45-9

Preface

The starting point for this study was a long-standing interest in Victorian 'model' villages. They are recognisable as architectural unities but whilst early villages, such as Swindon Railway Village (1840s) and Withnell Fold, Lancashire (1843), generally comprise unadorned functional buildings, some later communities display a level of decoration that I found surprising. They are works of art in their own right and, as with nineteenth-century paintings and sculpture, might, I thought, have messages embedded in the architecture for those with eyes to read them.

All architectural decoration is additional to the cost of construction and therefore embellishments are always carefully and deliberately chosen. The Victorians used the architecture of their buildings to make statements of civic pride and confidence and the decorative details of their grand buildings still beg us to understand them while the decoration of smaller buildings surely also has secrets to reveal.

This study attempts to unravel and explain the role of beautification and decoration in three nineteenth-century model communities which represent the three main architectural styles of the second half of the nineteenth century: Saltaire and Akroydon in West Yorkshire and Bedford Park in West London. The purposes of the communities were quite different one from the other which adds considerably to interest in the use of decorative detail.

I am very grateful for the enthusiastic assistance I received from the staff of the Shipley College Saltaire Archive, particularly Sandi Moore; from Roger Clarke, local historian in Saltaire; from the staff of Bankfield Museum, Halifax, particularly Jeff Wilkinson; from Kate Harrison, the key-holder of All Souls' Church, Haley Hill, Halifax, who opened the church specially for me and from the staff of the Victorian Society, particularly their honorary librarian, Jane Wainwright. Without their help, I would not have been able to access much of the reference material that I have used. I also wish to thank Alex Windscheffel of Royal Holloway, University of London for his patient advice and guidance, and Peter, my husband, for his constant encouragement.

Victoria Cross (detail),
Akroydon

Introduction

The three communities discussed in this book – Saltaire, Akroydon and Bedford Park – were different from each other in concept and represent developments in architectural style during the second half of the nineteenth century. This study illustrates the changes in tastes between 1850 and 1890 and provides a comparative view of the purposes to which architectural decoration was put. Saltaire, built between 1851 and 1876 on the outskirts of Bradford, is predominantly Italianate in style; Akroydon, built between 1855 and 1876 (with later additions) on the edge of Halifax, is Gothic while Bedford Park, built between 1875 and 1891 at Turnham Green, West London, is largely in the so-called Queen Anne Revival style. They were all referred to as 'utopian' by commentators of their time suggesting the idealistic and visionary nature of each. As precursors to the Garden City movement, all three were of significance in the development of housing for working people, both in Britain and abroad, throughout the twentieth century.

'Aesthetics', the branch of philosophy dealing with the nature and perception of the beautiful here refers to the interpretation of beauty by the creators of the three communities and also to the purposes to which that perceived beauty was put. In reference to the nineteenth century, the term is generally associated with the Aesthetic Movement, whose declared ethos, seen by many as excessive and affected, was the pursuit of beauty. It was at its height between 1875 and 1885, a period when many people moved away from the ornate High Victorian styles and consciously sought beauty in simpler more naturally-derived forms. It affected art in all its manifestations including architecture, furniture, interior decoration and clothing and had strong links with the Arts and Crafts Movement, inspired by William Morris. However, in the previous decades, people had also been looking for ways to reassert the beautiful in urban environments in order to relieve the dehumanising ugliness of industrial development.

Decorative embellishments were integral to most civic developments, conveying messages of power and pride, and ornate private buildings were a means of achieving lasting recognition for their wealthy owners. A characteristic of Saltaire, Akroydon and Bedford Park was that humble dwellings and public buildings erected for working people were also decorated.

Despite their differences, the aesthetics of each community developed from the realisation that in the rush to provide new dwellings for those working in the new industrial towns, decorative considerations had been overlooked. The creators of these villages had the vision to understand that, for people at all levels of society, a decent and attractive home in pleasant surroundings was conducive to a contented existence which led to a more productive population. The creators also understood that decoration provided themselves with ample means to make their own lasting personal statements. Buildings, like paintings, could give information and often a moral message as well. Furthermore, artistic symbolism became highly developed, allowing the expression of ideas independent of literacy.

In carrying out the study, it became apparent that the aesthetic aspects of these communities reveal much, not only of the ideas and tastes of the time, but of the ideas and ambitions of the patrons who funded the developments and also of the architects they employed. It also became clear that the beliefs and motivations of all the creators (patrons and architects) were integral to the design details of the communities studied. However, these aesthetic details are consistently glossed over in accounts of the communities. This study makes its purpose to attempt to reveal the hidden significance of the aesthetic details.

Biographical details of the men who created these three communities are limited to details relevant to the aesthetics of the villages, and both patrons and architects are assessed in relation to the planning and architectural detail of each village. Many new pictures illustrate how ideas were translated into the construction of these communities.

1

The Italianate Aesthetics of Saltaire

Sir Titus Salt and Saltaire

Saltaire, three miles north of Bradford, was the idea of Sir Titus Salt (1803–76) and was built for his mill workers. Salt was the son of a West Riding farmer turned wool-dealer and was brought up in a strictly Nonconformist home. He left Batley Grammar School at the age of 17 and began his working life in a competitor wool business, joining his father's firm in 1824 as a wool buyer. He travelled widely within England to wool sales and to auctions of imported fleeces in London and Liverpool but it is unlikely that he ever travelled outside Britain.

In 1833 on a business visit to Liverpool, Salt discovered in a warehouse a batch of rejected alpaca fleece. This fibre had never been successfully processed and his subsequent purchase of a consignment in 1836 and personal development of processing techniques laid the foundation of his fortune. By the time of his father's death in 1843, the business owned five spinning and weaving mills in Bradford.

Salt was an outstanding businessman but he was also committed to philanthropy, which extended well beyond Saltaire. He became the wealthiest man in Bradford and was prominent in local politics as a magistrate and, in 1848, as Bradford's second mayor. Through this public involvement, he became deeply aware of the poverty and social problems in the rapidly growing city and became a leader for social reform. In 1859, he was elected Liberal Member of Parliament for Bradford. He was no orator, speaking seldom in public and then only briefly. According to his friend, the Rev. R. Balgarnie, who wrote the first biography of Salt, 'His words were

1.1 1 Saltaire, belevedere-capped ventilation tower on the mill

always few, often painfully few'.[1] He made no parliamentary speeches and resigned his seat in 1861, due possibly to ill-health or, as suggested in *The Graphic* in 1877, 'in order that he might again join his beloved workpeople in Yorkshire'.[2] He read few books and wrote little and was described by Balgarnie as 'plodding'.[3] Nothing written by Salt survives so his interests and motivations have to be deduced from the writings of others and from other indicators, including the buildings themselves in Saltaire.

Salt understood the commercial wisdom of concentrating his mill business onto one site. He selected an ideal location, 'one of the most beautiful and picturesque to be found in the neighbourhood of Bradford'[4] in a valley, served by river, canal, railway and turnpike road where the prevailing winds would blow smoke away from the proposed development. The mill was the first building constructed but Salt realised from the outset that if his workers lived around the mill, he would be able to exert greater control than if they lived elsewhere. He also understood that well-housed workers were likely to be more productive and the idea of a complete community formed early. Saltaire was remarkable in its own time for the completeness of the community and for the architectural unity of its buildings. Salt never lived

1.2 The Salt crest on the tympanum of the central school building. It is supported by alpacas, the source of Salt's wealth, to serve as a reminder of Sir Titus himself

in Saltaire, although Balgarnie suggests that at an early stage he planned to do so.[5] However, the village was his obsession, to the virtual exclusion of pursuits followed by other wealthy people.

The Salt family had no hereditary coat of arms, being of too low birth. As his wealth and influence increased, Titus Salt felt a need for such an aristocratic emblem and he sent representatives to London to research coats of arms. The crest of an unrelated Salt family was found and adapted for him and the right to use it was granted in 1847.[6] It is 'azure, a chevron indented between two mullets (five pointed stars) and a demi ostrich holding in the beak a horse shoe in base Or (gold)'.[7]

In heraldic terms, azure indicates truth and loyalty while gold shows generosity and elevation of the mind. A chevron signifies protection for those who have accomplished some work of faithful service; the stars indicate divine quality bestowed from above; the ostrich (an infrequently used heraldic symbol) stands for willing obedience and serenity. The horseshoe is for good luck and protection. Although all these qualities can be related to Salt, and were plainly intended to be seen in this way, they were not specific to him, which led to the introduction sometimes of one or two supporting alpacas, representing the source of his wealth **(1.2)**.

Salt was created a baronet in 1869, when a hand was inserted in the upper middle of his crest.[8] This was intended to represent a pledge of faith and sincerity – presumably in relation to what he was seeking to achieve in his philanthropic works at Saltaire and elsewhere. His adopted Latin motto, *'Quid Non Deo Juvante'* ('What can a man not do with God's help'), underlined the centrality of religion to his life.[9, 10]

The entire village was designed by Lockwood and Mawson, a Bradford architectural partnership. Henry Lockwood, the senior partner, had been a pupil in the London firm of P F Robinson, which had a reputation for classically inspired designs. He joined with William Mawson in 1849 and 'quickly achieved an extraordinary near-monopoly of the town's biggest civic commissions'.[11] Although they worked in a variety of styles, their characteristic style was a 'more than competent Italianate, which was supplemented by efficiently derivative Gothic when required.'[12] They designed most of Bradford's prestigious buildings as well as buildings in other cities, including London. The stone carving in the village, much of it very ornate, was the responsibility of Yorkshireman Thomas Milnes.

Salt began negotiations to build Saltaire, 'the exemplar of industrial Italianate' in 1851.[13] The decision to build in Italianate style was probably that of Salt himself: the association of Gothic architecture with the Anglican Church would have made it unthinkable as his style of choice. Moreover,

1.3 The Saltaire Mill with centrally placed belvedere-capped towers. Practical as well as decorative, they made a virtue of the ventilation shafts from the toilets

classically inspired buildings had a solid and confident appearance and, in their associations with the empires of Greece and Rome, spoke of power, civilisation and learning – qualities of fundamental importance to Salt. It is unlikely that Lockwood, equally competent in other styles,[14] would recommend a style whose popularity was already passing.[15] From the 1850s onwards, the style tended to be limited to civic buildings and banks: Italianate domestic buildings were unusual. Salt himself would have been strongly influenced by architecture seen while travelling on business. In particular, the developing grandeur of the classical temple design of St George's Hall in Liverpool, begun in 1841, cannot have failed to make a lasting impression on him.

The mill

When Salt commissioned the building of the mill, he queried Lockwood's estimated costing of £100,000, asking if it would not be possible to build it for less. 'Not in the way you want it to be done,' was apparently the answer, whereupon he agreed immediately.[16] It is likely that Lockwood quickly drew

13

1.4 The administration section of Salt's mill. The rounded windows and keystones provide more decoration here than on the exterior of the rest of the mill

conclusions regarding Salt's relative ignorance of architecture and other cultural refinements, coupled with his paymaster's overwhelming desire to make his lasting mark in the expanding city of Bradford. He realised that he was being offered the opportunity to create not only a memorial to Salt but also his own memorial. Salt accepted Lockwood's costing and so began an association of around 25 years, during which time Saltaire was built – a monument not only to Titus Salt himself but also to his architects.

In the year of Salt's death, William Cudworth, a local writer, described the community:

> Saltaire has before now been likened to a commercial Utopia. However daring a flight of imagination this may seem, yet to our mind we have a fairly-realised Utopia even in manufacturing Saltaire. As a town – and especially as a manufacturing town – it is a marvel of cleanliness, cheerfulness and beauty … nothing is done by halves at Saltaire… The massive yet elegant factory, the graceful Italian church, the noble educational institute and school premises opposite, and the cheerful-looking almshouses all form a harmonious whole.[17]

It is clear that in the perception of 'Utopia', the visual appearance of

1.5 'An ornament to the place': the Venetian campanile-style chimney of the 1868 mill extension

1.6 The original dining room with the Salt crest above the door – a ready reminder of the master at meal times

the community was seen as remarkable. The mill, 'a symmetrical building, beautiful to look at'[18] opened in 1853, and was the first textile factory in the world where all processes were brought together in one building. Its size alone was ground-breaking[19] but the idea to clothe it in an Italianate shell associated the mill with the confident civic buildings that were being erected in the burgeoning northern towns rather than with industrial buildings. It was 'supposedly modelled on Osborne House, Queen Victoria's residence on the Isle of Wight'[20] in what would have been a deliberate attempt on Salt's part to associate with the royal family. His early ambition to purchase part of the Crystal Palace for use as a weaving shed after the 1851 Great Exhibition (Salt and Lockwood visiting London specifically to do so) would have further reinforced this attempted link and Salt must have been disappointed when Lockwood convinced him that the structure was not sufficiently substantial to withstand the vibrations from machinery The rejection of the Crystal Palace allowed Lockwood to make his own proposals.

The mill was built of local stone ashlar with a decorated mill chimney and two square towers capped with belvederes on the central part of the symmetrical frontage. Design was put to practical use here, in ventilating the toilets underneath, allowing them to be situated conveniently rather than kept out of sight **(1.3)**.[21] The administration section of the building was more decorated than elsewhere, with rustication, round-headed windows and an undecorated keystone **(1.4)**. Nikolaus Pevsner described the decoration as 'feeble Italianate trimmings' and saw the mill chimney 'in the form of a starved campanile',[22] although contemporaries, amazed at the village they saw taking shape, were hugely enthusiastic.

The size of the mill was intended to inspire awe. Beautification through architectural detail allowed it to masquerade as a grand civic building, thus elevating the role of industry in society. In 1868 an extension to the mill opened on the north side of the canal. According to Balgarnie: 'The erection of a new chimney was objected to as detracting from the view … Mr Salt's reply was, "I'll make it an ornament to the place." '[23] So its chimney was disguised to look like the campanile of the church of Santa Maria Gloriosa in Venice, taken from a contemporary design manual: Rawlinson's '*Designs for Furnaces, Factories and Tall Chimneys*' **(1.5)**.[24]

1.7 Overlookers' houses in George Street, designed so that the residents might enjoy a morally improving vista of the church

1.8 A triple-arcaded window of the 1860s on Titus Street achieved a more picturesque appearance than in previous housing

The works' dining room was completed shortly after the mill. Situated opposite the mill, it is a simple Italianate stone structure, the main entrance embellished with the Salt coat of arms. With this simple item of beautification, Salt reassured himself that his employees would be reminded of his benevolence whenever they took a meal **(1.6)**.

Housing in Saltaire

The style of the housing, 'an economic Italianate style',[25] was derived from that of the mill. Constructed in stone of the same colour as the mill, the houses were begun in 1854 and were built in several phases. They are of different qualities, 'monotonous'[26] with varying amounts of 'Italianate trim'.[27] In *The Homes of the Working Classes*, (1866), James Hole published drawings, apparently provided by Titus Salt, of overlooker's cottages and workmen's cottages in Saltaire. [28] There are no other surviving drawings so even though Hole's drawings are not an exact match to any in Saltaire, the view was perpetuated that Salt and his architects intended the amount of

1.9 (Opposite) Saltaire Congregational (now United Reformed) Church of 1859: one of England's finest Nonconformist churches

decoration, including the presence or otherwise of a small garden, to indicate the status of the head of household in the mill hierarchy. However, a recent study of Saltaire by Neil Jackson, Jo Lintonbon and Bryony Staples suggests that this was an unsuccessful aesthetic intention: they argue convincingly that total family income rather than status determined the type of house that was rented.[29]

The first houses built were on William Henry Street and George Street and are still referred to locally as overlookers' houses. Taking their styling from the mill, the two-storey houses had round-headed arches with plain keystones framing the front door and the ground-floor window: 'characteristic of what is known as the Tuscan or Italian villa style',[30] in a clear attempt to link both houses and their occupants to the mill. The houses had small front gardens and the monotony of the terraces was broken by three-storey pavilions at each end and in the middle – the whole having a simple but pleasing symmetrical appearance. The vista of the church at the end of the road was part of the morally improving intention of the aesthetic detailing **(1.7)**.

The first building contract apparently ran into financial difficulty, possibly through the cost of building uphill in order to achieve vistas of the mill and church while seeking to achieve Italianate symmetry. When the second contract began 'the architectural quality if not the material quality, of the houses reduced'[31] into the plain houses on Amelia Street, Fanny Street and Herbert Street. Here there were no gardens and windows and doors had a plain lintel. Subsequent houses were even plainer being deprived of top-lights over the front door and individual corbel brackets were replaced by a continuous gutter tray. No matter how simple the styling, however, the architects managed to maintain the aesthetic of symmetry required in classically inspired architecture. Most of the later 1850s houses followed the plain style except, for reasons of aesthetic cohesion, continuations of existing streets. Doors and windows in the new houses in George Street had square window and door hoods in the Italian Palazzo style.

Housing from 1860 onwards was generally more aesthetically pleasing. Ornamentation increased again, not necessarily due to greater generosity of funding but, as the houses were now built along the contours, less needed to be spent on accommodating to the changes in gradient. A more picturesque appearance was achieved by returning to the rounded-window style, repeating previously used details and introducing three-light first-floor windows for the first time **(1.8)**.

The last building contract, in 1866, included superior housing in Albert Road and formed the western edge of the village. It included the only houses in pairs or groups of four among otherwise terraced housing. Locally known as managers' houses, they were significantly larger than other village houses and had spacious gardens. These houses combine architectural styles and include Italian Palazzo details as well as Doric columns and pilasters with stiff-leaf capitals topping the columns separating paired windows. Introduced for the first time was 'Ruskinian Gothic' polychrome on round-arched windows, styling favoured by Prince Albert and 'it is possible that the architects were paying homage to the Consort in the use of this Romanesque style.'[32] This may indeed have been a mark of respect following his death in 1861 but it was also a means of Lockwood and Mawson maintaining their professional integrity. Through Ruskin's influence, architectural taste by the 1860s had moved towards Gothic and as an architectural practice, whatever their patron's views, they needed to be seen to be abreast of current fashion even if they were still building in an older style at Saltaire.

The village housing programme was completed by 1869, with houses fronting the main road, wedged into awkwardly shaped sites. Nonetheless, attractive detailing ensured a good foretaste of Salt's village from the main road.

Saltaire's public buildings

The first of Saltaire's public buildings was the Congregational Church, sited immediately opposite the mill (1.9). Of very unusual design, it was begun in 1858, 'in opulent Italianate style with semi-circular portico and domed cylindrical tower'[33] and, in Pevsner's view, 'the only aesthetically successful building at Saltaire'.[34] It was completed and opened in April 1859 and remains one of England's finest nineteenth-century Nonconformist churches and Lockwood and Mawson's most successful building.[35] Its Corinthian portico and domed tower with attractive iron grilles between smaller Corinthian columns give it a strikingly unusual appearance although the similar St Mary's Church, Banbury, of 1797, may well have been Lockwood's inspiration.

The lavish interior decoration of the church is surprising for a Nonconformist church but for Salt, it was a unique opportunity both to communicate his commitment to Congregationalism and to construct an opulent memorial to himself (1.10). Blue scagliola pillars topped with leafy gold painted capitals line the walls and two magnificent ormolu, gilt and cut glass chandeliers hang from the roof. Blue and gold, the main colours of the Salt crest, subtly reinforced associations with the founder.

Inside the church, there was a decorative balcony for the use of the Salt family although they apparently never used it, preferring to sit with the

1.10 The lavishly decorated interior of Saltaire Church. The blue and gold of the decoration were the main colours of the Salt crest

main congregation on the few occasions when they attended services there. Nonetheless, situated as it was at the back of the church above the main door, it symbolised Salt's presence, even when he was not there **(1.11)**.

There are numerous references to Salt incorporated into the decoration of the church: his initials are formed into finials behind the choir stalls, his monogram is repeated on the frieze along the top of the walls **(1.12)** and a large scrolled 'S' is carved into the end of each pew – repeated reminders to employees of their employer's munificence **(1.13)**.

The square family mausoleum, on the south side of the church, completed in 1861, with a domed roof on Corinthian pilasters, was designed to be an ever-present reminder of the Salt family **(1.14)**. It was full of materials and decorations that clearly stated Salt's wealth: it 'contains a beautiful full-length female figure, emblematic of the Resurrection, in pure Italian marble … other rare examples of tablet work adorn the walls'.[36]

Although a staunch Congregationalist, Salt was tolerant of other denominations and in 1866 provided the land for a Wesleyan Methodist chapel (demolished 1970). Designed by Lockwood and Mawson, 'in the

1.11 The Salt family balcony at the rear of Saltaire Church reminded churchgoers of the Salts even when they were not in church

1.12 Saltaire Church: the Salt monogram on the frieze along the top of the walls

1.13 Saltaire Church: a large 'S' carved into the end of each pew

Venetian Gothic style with a three bay two storey gabled centrepiece and Venetian Gothic (very 'Ruskinian') arches. The façade had … arched windows with keystones typical of the village.'[37] Otherwise the building was of a simple box design – a typical plain Wesleyan 'preaching-box' reflecting the congregation's tight budget **(1.15)**.

The Italianate factory school (or 'schools' as boys and girls were educated separately), 'designed to be exemplars of their type'[38] were opened in 1868. Set back from the village's main street with a garden in front, they were remarkably ornate for an institution for the children of factory hands **(1.16)**. Built of rusticated ashlar, the central building is crowned by a bell turret 'with figures of children holding instruments of instruction',[39] plainly intended to inspire the young pupils **(1.17)**.

Colonnades supported by Corinthian columns linked the centre to both sides. Salt decorative devices embellished the front of the building: the tympanum of the central gable holds a carving of the Salt crest flanked by two alpacas and the monograms of Salt and his wife, Caroline, decorate those of the side buildings **(1.18)**.

Forty-five almshouses 'resembling Italian villas',[40] including a small chapel, were opened in 1870 around the landscaped Alexandra Square. Lockwood and Mawson, introduced some two-storey sections for aesthetic interest in defiance of Salt's preference for a single-storey only. However, the central two-storey building was surmounted not only by a decorative bell-turret but also by Salt monograms, which must have mollified their paymaster.

Apart from the reminders of the founder's benevolence, the almshouses have an abundance of attractive decorative detailing, much of it Gothic, 'reflecting the virtues of a traditional England where charitable paternalism

1.14 Saltaire Church: the Salt mausoleum served as a reminder for all time of the creator of the community

1.15 Saltaire: the Wesleyan Methodist Chapel, a simple box design with a Venetian Gothic façade (*Shipley College Saltaire Archive*)

1.16 Saltaire School: a remarkably ornate building for working class children (*Shipley College Saltaire Archive*)

1.17 Saltaire School: the bell-turret decorated with figures of children holding instruments of instruction, intended to inspire the children of the factory workers

was seen as having sustained the fabric of society' **(1.19)**.[41] They are the most attractive buildings in the village and an expression of the greater freedom the architects assumed, twenty years after beginning work on the village. In the same development and in the same style, was a purpose-built hospital with an alpaca-topped crest adorning the tympanum.

The Club and Institute, the most richly ornamented building in the village and the costliest of all the public buildings, opened in 1871 **(1.20)**. It was intended for the moral and physical welfare of the community, and was located immediately opposite the school. Although Pevsner described the main entrance as 'a hideous richly Baroque portal',[42] contemporary commentators, such as the local writer William Cudworth, were enthusiastic: 'The palatial and beautifully proportioned façade at once arrests the attention of the visitor'.[43] Inside were lecture theatres, a library, reading rooms, classrooms, a gymnasium, a billiards room and a school of art. According to Cudworth, 'It was like a university college'.[44] There is little doubt that, in providing education for both young people and adults, it was considered one of the most complete centres of education in England at the time.[45]

1.18 The monogram of Titus Salt on the gable on one side of the school. The monogram of his wife, Caroline, filled the other side gable

1.19 The Saltaire almshouses, where Salt was persuaded that Gothic styling, reflecting traditional English virtues, was the appropriate style

1.20 Saltaire Club and Institute, shortly after opening (*Shipley College Saltaire Archive*)

Each side of the gateway two stone lions, carved by Thomas Milnes, faced two more outside the school. According to Balgarnie, 'these are works of art, superior, in the estimation of many, to those at the base of the Nelson monument in Trafalgar Square; indeed they were originally designed for that monument'.[46] As another link with London, Salt was surely delighted to acquire these sculptures when Edwin Landseer's lions were preferred for Trafalgar Square. They 'put a stamp of majesty on the building, and, indeed, on the entire street' **(1.21)**.[47]

The building was set back from the road facing the school. Above the main door was the Salt coat of arms, now with the hand included, proclaiming Salt's baronetcy, granted in 1869. These were flanked by Milnes' sculptures representing Science (with a retort and scales) and Art (with a palette and brush), as an exhortation to further study **(1.22)**. Surmounting the whole building over the entrance is a pyramidal tower with a spire, decorated by Corinthian columns and intricate carving.

The Institute is richly decorated with carvings amongst which the front second-floor windows bear the only carved keystones in the whole community. Decorated with a head, most seem to represent classical deities, as was common contemporary practice on such keystones. No surviving identification record survives but an attempt has been made to distinguish

1.21 One of the stone lions sculpted by Thomas Milnes and, according to contemporary writers, originally intended for Trafalgar Square. Their location outside the places of learning in Saltaire made a strong statement of connection to London, its culture and learning, and made Saltaire vicariously a part of the hub of the British Empire

1.22 The Salt crest above the main door to the Institute. A hand is inserted into Salt's adopted coat of arms, signifying his recent baronetcy. Sculptures representing Science and Art support the crest, creating a spectacularly opulent entrance to this palace of learning

1.23 The carved keystones on Saltaire Institute, including an unexpected grinning bacchanalian head on the far right

them.[48] From this, it can be deduced that they were carefully chosen, both in relation to the building and to the community itself. They include (from left to right) Juno, who, as protector of marriage and women, represented one aspect of social reform which was so important to Salt; Venus, the Roman goddess of beauty, characterises the whole Saltaire development, the beauty of which was often remarked upon; Jupiter or Zeus, as king of the gods determining all human affairs, perhaps represented Salt himself; Mars, as patron of those who worked the land recalls Salt's origins; Hercules, who achieved immortality through performing challenging tasks served as an example to Salt's employees to strive to achieve their best; Minerva, Roman goddess of the arts and trades, can be seen as mentor to the Institute and to the village itself.

It is thought other heads were members of Salt's family. Whether deities or Salt family, the first residents of Saltaire would have recognised them and, yet again, they would have been reminded of Salt's munificence. All the heads have serious expressions except the last which wears a vacant grin. It is of a bacchanalian character and in a community where no public house was permitted, an allusion to the drinking of alcohol is wholly unexpected.

1.24 The Institute main hall: richly decorated restored ceiling detail

Very likely the architects placed it as a joke, counting on the fact that Salt would not notice it at the end of the row of heads **(1.23)**.

The interior of the Institute was richly decorated, 'the eye being delighted with … the exquisite gracefulness and harmony of the embellishments',[49] making it a fitting venue for the entertainment of high-ranking guests and to further inspire mill employees who attended for educational purposes **(1.24)**. The Institute had the appearance of a small town hall and it is possible that this is what Salt intended it to be:

> Correspondence with the General Board of Health indicated that officials of the Board had led Salt to believe his township would be a new and entirely separate local government district. He was very annoyed when he discovered that this was not the case and that he would have to pay rates to the Shipley Board of Health, the local authority for the district.[50]

Had Salt achieved his separate township, the Institute could have been transformed into a very respectable town hall. If this had occurred, the Congregational Sunday School, described as 'an afterthought of 1875-6'[51] and the last building constructed in the village could well have assumed the

2

The Gothic Aesthetics of Akroydon

Edward Akroyd and Akroydon

Akroydon was built in 'Pennine Gothic style',[1] the creation of Edward Akroyd (1810-87). Built next to an Akroyd family mill, it was not primarily intended as housing for the mill workers but was an attempt at social engineering. Akroyd tried to create a community containing all strata of society, as in medieval towns, never intending to own the housing himself. He devised a mortgage scheme for owner occupation rendering the development innovative and different from the majority of other nineteenth-century industrial housing projects.

Born into a wealthy mill-owning family, Akroyd, like Salt, was raised in a Nonconformist home and educated locally. Why he attended Barkisland Endowed School, a Church of England school, is unknown, but it was to have a profound influence on his later life. He was known as 'a man of taste and culture, who had travelled abroad and knew all the Continental art galleries'[2] suggesting that he took the Grand Tour of Europe, as did the sons of many manufacturers.[3]

On the death of their father, Jonathan, in 1847, Akroyd and his brother inherited James Akroyd and Sons, a business founded by their grandfather. His brother retired from the business in 1853, and Edward 'became the owner of probably the country's largest worsted manufacturer'.[4] Like Salt, whom he knew well, he was appalled by the social conditions resulting from rapid urban development and became committed to improving conditions for his employees and improving the lives of his fellow men. Akroyd and Salt had witnessed the unrest of the late 1830s and early 1840s and remembered the riots and bloodshed of the Plug Plot of 1842 when troops were required to prevent the storming of the Akroyd mill. Increasing business prosperity meant that Akroyd could pursue political interests: he held numerous prominent public positions including magistrate (1849), Deputy Lieutenant of the West Riding and Liberal MP for Halifax (1865-74). He trod an independent path within the Whig/Liberal grouping in parliament and in the 1870s attempted to form a cross-party alliance known as the Constitutional Party. By 1874, his views differed significantly from those of his party, the electorate of Halifax had lost confidence in him and he was replaced by his local textiles rival, John Crossley.

His philanthropic projects were many and intended to promote stability in an economically divided society. He founded the first Working Men's College outside London (1855) and was the 'principal promoter'[5] in the setting up of the Yorkshire Penny Savings Bank in 1859, to encourage saving amongst working people. He became a member the Odd Fellows and the Foresters 'as a token of respect for those societies, which were admirably managed by working men.'[6] He was known as Colonel Edward Akroyd from 1870, the title deriving from his leadership of a volunteer unit and retained in an honorary capacity after his retirement.

Akroyd obtained the granting of a coat of arms in 1855, to be borne by himself and descendants and by the descendants of his late father.[7] It was derived, after research on his behalf, from the arms of Akroyd ancestors of two and a half centuries earlier. The hereditary motif was a stag's head and the heraldic connotations of this motif – peace, harmony, and fighting only if provoked – suited Akroyd's intentions well. Strength and fortitude are symbolised by the stag's antlers, qualities that Akroyd embodied later in his life as he tried to make his ideas understood against increasing opposition. A wreath of oak leaves was added in allusion to the meaning of the name Akroyd or 'oak royd', a clearing amidst a clump of oak trees.[8] The connotations of great age (his ancestry) and strength connected with oaks also suited his purposes well. The acorn symbol, which Akroyd used widely in Akroydon, alluded additionally to continuous growth and fertility, which related perfectly to Akroyd's ambitions for his model community.

His motto was '*In veritae victoria*' ('Victory in truth'). This fitted well to his self-confident beliefs but in the Latin there was also a clear allusion to the Queen, which underlined his strong belief in the monarchy.

Unlike Salt, Akroyd was a good communicator. He spoke confidently in public and published his ideas on various topics.[9] He had a strong personal interest in architecture and when MP was a member of George Gilbert Scott's 'Spring Gardens Sketching Club' in London.[10] He developed strong views about improving housing for the working class and published his own ideas in 1862: *On Improved Dwellings for the Working Class: A Plan for Building them in Connection with Benefit Building Societies*, in the hope of persuading others to follow his example in providing better housing for the working classes.

Akroydon was Edward Akroyd's second 'model' village, having built, between 1849 and 1853, the mildly Gothic village of Copley near Halifax for employees of his Copley mill. Pre-dating Saltaire, it undoubtedly influenced Salt's planning of Saltaire. Akroyd was disappointed to find that employees were unwilling to pay higher rents for superior housing so he began to formulate alternative ways of assisting wage-earning people to acquire better living conditions. Several architects and designers were involved in the creation of Akroydon although none had the personal involvement of Lockwood and Mawson at Saltaire. Certainly none of those associated with the aesthetics of the community were linked to Akroydon for as long as the Bradford firm were to Saltaire. Decorative work was carried out by artist craftsmen of national standing.

In common with others 'searching for stability and a sense of reason in a very unstable and rapidly changing Victorian age',[11] he began looking back to an idealised medieval society, where the building style was Gothic. With strong connotations of liberty, the choice of this style:

> was not simply an aesthetic choice of an architectural style romantically recalling a fanciful medieval past. It was a powerful political statement; it was intended to be a vision to guide the new age … . Gothic was intended to be a symbol of a new class harmony, even if it was to be within a hierarchical, feudal, social order … [led by] the new [industrial] aristocrats, like Edward Akroyd.[12]

Gothic was the only appropriate architectural style for Akroyd whose second village was to establish a self-help facility for working people. He wanted to create a new 'English' society of independent, educated and democratic working men[13] and expected others to follow his example.

Beginning the building of Akroyd's dream

Edward Akroyd's first venture was to safeguard the memory of the Akroyd family by building a family mausoleum. In 1855 he bought five fields on Haley Hill, close to Bankfield, his own home since 1838, for the construction of the village. He immediately commissioned Halifax architects Mallinson and Healey to construct a burial ground and mortuary chapel in what was to become All Souls' Burial Ground. The entrance to the cemetery was

2.2 The Gothic-style entrance to the burial ground announced the beginning of Akroyd's experiment in recreating a medieval town

marked by a sexton's house and a Gothic-style arch, surmounted by a gable and cross **(2.2)**. The arch bears Akroyd's stag's head crest together with his motto.

This early application of the stag motif was a statement of his own proud self-confidence at the outset of his scheme. The chapel, according to a wall inscription, 'erected by his sons Edward and Henry as an offering of filial reverence and affection':[14]

> was an elaborate Early English structure, with altar and font in Caen stone, carved oak seats, floors and east wall covered in Minton tiles, and stained glass by George Hedgeland [1825–98] and Clayton and Bell. Off it opened the 'monumental chapel', with a stone vault on Derbyshire

marble pillars. In the centre was the full-length effigy of Jonathan Akroyd, executed in Rome in 1863 by the Leeds sculptor Joseph Gott.[15]

The Akroyd arms and motto were repeated four times in the floor tiles and the Akroyd armorial shield was included in the east window.[16] This, the first building of the new village, was clearly more than 'filial reverence and affection': it was a powerful announcement to prospective inhabitants of the village and to posterity of the identity of the creator of the community.

In 1855, after considering several architects,[17] Akroyd commissioned George Gilbert Scott, by then at the height of his fame, to design a large new Anglican church opposite his mill on Haley Hill, together with a vicarage. By this time, Akroyd had embraced the Established Church, believing it was the foundation of the stable society he aimed to recreate.

All Souls' Church

On the same day as the consecration of the cemetery in 1856, Akroyd laid the foundation stone for All Souls' Church, amidst great ceremony, having already been instrumental in the creation of the parish of Haley Hill (2.1). All Souls' Church was consecrated in 1859, 'in plan and style ... the legitimate descendant of the old English Pointed parish churches.'[18] London-based Scott already had a reputation as an eminent Gothic architect and by choosing to entrust his church to him, Akroyd was not only clearly stating his own preference for Gothic but was also showing that his own ambitions went beyond West Yorkshire and that his church was to be ranked with the best on the national stage. It is likely that Scott was chosen precisely because he did not have a clear personal style – his churches were not all easily identifiable as 'Scott' churches. Akroyd must have envisaged (erroneously as history has shown) that the Haley Hill church could therefore be designed to be for ever associated with himself – the church's patron – rather than with its architect.

Akroyd made it clear that he was prepared to pay for the very best in his church. For Scott, this must have been an irresistible opportunity and he 'created one of the crowning jewels of Victorian Gothic, superb in outline and massing, a seamless blend of French and Italian influences with English Decorated architecture, and laden with intense decoration from the very best artists of the day'.[19]

The exterior is unusually impressive. Its location on ground that slopes steeply to the south and west and a soaring spire (2.3) make it particularly commanding. Stepped buttresses add to the richness of effect, as well as statues and opulent decoration on the spire. The tympanum of the great

2.3 All Souls' Church: the soaring spire took the epitome of human decorative skills heavenward

2.4 All Souls' Church: the chancel, richly decorated with carved stonework, ironwork and magnificent stained glass

2.5 All Souls' Church: carved roundels of saints peering down on the nave

west door was richly decorated with a carved figure of Christ accompanied by two angels and a text.

The interior was 'full of colour, combining painted decoration, polished granite, marble, mosaic and stained glass, all to designs by top craftsmen. The chancel **(2.4)** and monumental pulpit are … extravagant.'[20] The stone carvings, mainly by John Birnie Philip (1824-75), perhaps best known for his work on the frieze of the Albert Memorial, were especially rich. Figurative sculpture featured prominently, including unusual roundels of saints looking down from above the arches of the nave **(2.5)**.

Native plants, particularly those found in Yorkshire were also represented abundantly among the carvings **(2.6)**[21] and much coloured marble was used — most strikingly on the pulpit **(2.7, 2.8)**. The stonework was to be an exuberant celebration of the botanical and geological bounty of God's Creation and a manifestation of Akroyd's pride in the county of his birth. It also gave a statement that Akroyd was abreast of contemporary issues — in this instance, the new science of geology.

There was also fine wood carving on the pews and in the choir stalls. The floor tiles were by Minton and became richer the nearer they were to the altar. The rich tracery of the windows contained much stained glass

2.6 All Souls' Church: carvings of native plants, particularly from Yorkshire, are in rich profusion, emphasising Akroyd's pride in his native county

2.7 (left) and 2.8 (above) All Souls' Church: the pulpit included much coloured marble in celebration of the geological bounty of God's creation and of the contemporary fascination in the new science of geology

2.9 All Souls' Church: one of the many windows, rich in tracery and stained glass, that contribute significantly to the opulent atmosphere of the church

mostly by John Hardman (1812-67) of Birmingham, (considered amongst his finest) and by Clayton and Bell **(2.9)**.

Like Salt, Akroyd wanted to leave his own mark on the church but his means of doing so was more restrained than at Saltaire. The south chapel was designated the 'founder's chapel' with the Akroyd coat of arms in the centre of the floor. Tiles also carry the inscription: 'To the honour of God and the holy blessed and glorious Trinity this church was founded by Edward Akroyd, merchant and manufacturer of Halifax AD 1859'. Apart from this, reminders of him are limited: inside the south door, the heads on the hood stops inside the south door possibly represent Akroyd and his wife,[22] his coat of arms is placed above the south doorway and the west window by Hedgeland bears the Akroyd stag's head motif.

Apart from the founder's chapel, worshippers could easily have missed his personal references. Nonetheless, with the church Akroyd created, at huge expense and with great personal interest, the grandest of memorials to himself. Its dimensions increased in size as the building progressed, largely in an attempt to outshine the Congregational Church being built by his rival John Crossley, with All Souls' spire finally twelve inches higher than the one at Crossley's Church.[23]

The housing in Akroydon

George Gilbert Scott prepared the first designs of the village. This was his first venture into town planning and he may have tired of an unglamorous project compared to All Souls' Church as he handed the project to William Crossland, a Yorkshireman and one of his pupils. Some parts were then subcontracted to architects Mallinson and Healey.

Work began on the houses of Akroyd's idealised society in 1861. The plan for owner occupation was derived from an earlier scheme, the Halifax Union Building Society. Akroyd assessed the earlier scheme as deficient although financially successful: in particular, the houses were 'devoid of architectural proportion and beauty, thereby indicating to me the mode in which I might work with them…'[24]

He continued in his publication on improved housing:

> My plan was simply this; – to purchase a suitable plot of land for a building site; to obtain designs from an able architect for building blocks of dwellings, eight or ten each… and to find parties who were willing to take up each successive block, forming themselves into a building association for this purpose, in connection with the Halifax Permanent Benefit Building Society which would advance three fourths of the capital required. I was fortunate in finding a plot of land in my own locality.[25]

This arrangement freed Akroyd from paying for the houses himself and left his funds available to finance the purchase of land, the building of roads and, importantly, the church and a village green or park. These were essential

2.10 Salisbury Place, where most front doors are distinguished with a carved stone monogram

to Akroyd's scheme for an ideal English village, as were other communal facilities, including allotments, a cemetery, stables and a co-operative shop. In all the planned buildings, Akroyd would be able to indulge his taste for the decorative detail that he found so lacking in the earlier Halifax Union Building Society scheme.

In Akroyd's idealised concept of a medieval community, Akroydon was intended from the outset to have a mixture of housing with himself at the centre as squire since he believed a return to an earlier hierarchical village society was fundamental to creating a harmonious community.

The initial Gothic designs for the village had to be amended at an early stage, to Akroyd's annoyance. As part of his own planned democratisation of the community, the Akroydon Building Association, a committee of potential home owners, had been formed to address details of the development and they:

> battled stoutly against the Gothic for some time; although they liked the look of it, they considered it antiquated, inconvenient, wanting in light, and not adapted to modern requirements. The dormer windows

were supposed to resemble the style of almshouses and the independent workmen who formed the building association positively refused to accept this feature of the Gothic, which to their minds was degrading. This point I was obliged to concede.[26]

Akroyd allowed the omission of the dormers, on the understanding that there would be no further alterations or he would refuse funding for the infrastructure. When the plans were put before proposed shareholders in 1860, they were told that the improved dwellings were 'to awaken the innate taste for the beautiful in outline … that the design should be Gothic: simple, yet bold in detail'.[27] To mollify the shareholders he added:

> This type was adopted not solely for the gratification of my own taste, but because it is the original style of the parish of Halifax … retaining the best features of the Elizabethan domestic architecture. Intuitively this taste of our forefathers pleases the fancy, strengthens house and home attachment, entwines the present with the memory of the past, and promises, in spite of opposition and prejudice, to become the national style of modern, as it was of old England.[28]

Built of stone and roofed in slate, the first two blocks on Salisbury Place **(2.10)** were completed in 1862, 'presenting a neat, pleasing exterior'.[29]

2.11 Monograms over doors gave individuality and distinction to homes

2.12 (above) and 2.13 (below) Houses individualised by geometric and foliage motifs

2.14 Ripon Terrace, designed by James Mallinson of Mallinson and Healey. Even before William Crossland followed his master to London in 1870, other local architects were employed for some of the work of the Akroydon community

Akroyd felt vindicated regarding the design: 'their prejudices against the pointed style are now finally uprooted.'[30]

Furthermore, they were 'much gratified by one feature recently introduced, viz., the insertion of the owner's monogram or device, on a stone shield, placed above the door **(2.11)**, with the intent to give individuality and a mark of distinction to each dwelling.'[31]

Having their own memorial, and crafted in so durable a medium as stone, would have been a source of great pride to the first occupants. Its very permanence made it a curious concession but it would have had the effect of instilling enormous satisfaction in home-ownership.

Presumably the very permanence of these decorative devices was soon seen to be a problem as they do not appear on the later cottages, although a variety of motifs, including native foliage, were used to individualise later houses **(2.12, 2.13)**.

Writing for the Halifax Antiquarian Society in 2004, Aidan Whelan asserted: 'The village's Gothicness was not an architectural gloss; it was

51

2.15 On the co-operative store, Beverley Terrace, the first-floor window was the most distinctively designed window in the community

Gothic through and through, in its sociology, economics, art and politics. Even the roadways were named after Gothic cathedrals.'[32]

William Crossland moved to London in 1870, passing Akroydon work to local architect William Swinden Barber. By 1873, though, the first phase of almost 100 houses (of 350 planned) was complete including 2-64 Salisbury Place, 1-9 Beverley Terrace, 8-24 Chester Road and 1-22 York Terrace, to Crossland designs and 1-25 Ripon Terrace by James Mallinson of Mallinson and Healey **(2.14)**.

A co-operative store on the corner of Salisbury Place and Beverley Terrace was included in the first phase of building. Around a first floor window Crossland included a substantial stone carving proclaiming the name of the community, surmounted by Akroyd's stag's head and the date of its construction (1861) as well as a monogram, probably of the first shopkeeper **(2.15)**.

Edward Akroyd's home: Bankfield House

Akroyd himself lived as lord of the manor in Akroydon. His home, Bankfield House, originally a fairly modest eight-roomed house, was extensively enlarged in 1867-8 and, despite his views regarding the appropriateness of Gothic in the designs of his model communities, it was to a 'grand Italian Trecento to Quattrocento design'[33] by J B and W Atkinson of York, creating an imposing Italianate mansion **(2.16)**.

Italianate architecture would have had the same resonance for Akroyd as it did for Salt in making a confident statement of status, power and wealth. At a time when the new barons of industry were building themselves mansions mostly in a Gothic style, Italianate styling enabled him to distance himself from the 'nouveaux-riches' and associate himself with the landed class whose mansions, all built in an earlier era, were classically inspired and symbolised for him the social stability he sought to revive.

He had the interior of his mansion richly decorated. Archaeological discoveries in Italy had stimulated a fashion for motifs drawn from the classical civilisations, the use of such decoration denoting culture and learning. Akroyd had a magnificent marble entrance staircase created, lined with decorations inspired by Pompeian and Herculanean frescoes. It led to his banqueting hall with a richly decorated ceiling and to his library also with much decorative work.[34] The result was a confident statement of his personal status. The Akroyd arms were not carved into the mansion. Apparently the only self-references in the house were large stone acorns on

2.16 Akroyd's home, Bankfield House, was a grand Italianate mansion

2.17 A stag's head over the arch of the gateway to Akroyd's stables: as an element in the Akroyd coat of arms, it makes a clear reference to Akroyd himself

the gateposts of the main entrance and acorns as well as his own and his wife's initials carved onto a fireplace.

Described by Pevsner as 'sumptuous Gothic',[35] the stables were in contrast to the relative simplicity of the Gothic village housing. Opposite Akroyd's mansion, they were elaborate and castellated, with a stag's head over the archway leading into the yard. They reminded his grooms of his munificence every time they passed by and reminded everyone else that the stables belonged to the master (2.17).

Outdoor space

For Akroyd, allotments were an important ingredient in his concept of a self-sufficient community and, like Salt, he provided land for them within the village plan. He also provided the small Square Park – just 1.5 acres – in 1876. As at Saltaire, the park came late in the development. He too may have had qualms about providing space for large public assemblies as it was not a public park. Instead, each householder had a key in return for an annual subscription towards the upkeep of the park and, as a modest reminder of his benefaction, Akroyd had the gateposts capped with stone acorns and wreathed with stone oak leaves (**2.18**).

In the centre of the park was placed a richly carved monument known as the Victoria Cross, designed by W S Barber. It is in the style of the crosses erected by King Edward I after the death of his queen, Eleanor. The king had a memorial in this style erected at each of the places where his queen's

2.18 A gatepost in Square Park, capped with an acorn and wreathed with oak leaves, is another reference to Akroyd

2.19 Square Park and the Victoria Cross

body rested overnight as he brought her back to London from where she died near Lincoln in 1290. Of huge significance to Akroyd was the fact that Edward I was the first monarch after the Norman Conquest to attempt to create a parliament that was representative of the people. By association, the Eleanor Crosses themselves became linked with liberty and democracy.

Over the centuries the twelve Eleanor Crosses were damaged or completely destroyed and forgotten until Gothic Revivalists in the 1830s became interested in them. Among these Gothicists, the young George Gilbert Scott went to great lengths to rediscover what was left of the crosses and to sketch them and he used his sketches in his winning design for the Martyrs' Memorial in Oxford. The memorial was commissioned as a libertarian statement against the growth of Tractarianism in Oxford. Referencing back to Edward I, it had connotations of democracy under a benign monarchy. Scott's memorial styled on the Eleanor Crosses was therefore perfect in concept and it led to a new interest in these crosses as an architectural motif associated with medieval Gothic liberty.

Numerous monuments followed Scott's Oxford memorial, all of them making a statement of Protestantism, liberty and loyalty to the sovereign.

2.20 The Victoria Cross, a revival Eleanor Cross, modelled on George Gilbert Scott's Martyrs' Memorial in Oxford

Whelan's detailed account of the Victoria Cross for the Halifax Antiquarian Society emphasises the significance of Akroyd's choice of model: selecting the Eleanor Cross style for his monument in Square Park **(2.19)** was

2.21 The statue of a young Queen Victoria on the Victoria Cross

clearly an aesthetic choice that was highly politically charged.[36] This was no 'millionaire's garden folly or the sycophancy of a royalist ... [but] ... enduring political art'.[37]

The Victoria Cross **(2.20)** carried an inscription in black on gold mosaic on the south side underlining Akroyd's belief in the bond between Christianity and the monarchy and his own claim to local pre-eminence: 'Erected as a Monument of Christian reverence for the emblem of the cross; and of loyalty to our sovereign lady Queen Victoria by Edward Akroyd, the founder of Akroydon, 1875. Fear God, Honour the King.'

On the same side beneath a canopy were a sculpture of Queen Victoria by John Birnie Philip **(2.21)** and a small shield of the Akroyd arms. The Decorated Gothic style spoke of the liberty and creativity of medieval society and, by placing Victoria on Eleanor's plinth, he was arguing (at a time when concern was being raised over a rise in republicanism) for the centrality of the ancient monarchy to ensure a stable society. Furthermore, Victoria is depicted as a young woman, a not widow in her 50s – the 'embodiment of a noble Gothic ideal, a far cry from ... the stereotypes of later years'.[38] By creating the monument as a type of cross, Akroyd made clear his belief in the fundamental importance of the Established Church and by making it in the style of the Eleanor crosses, he referenced the origins of representative democracy. The industrial neo-feudalism of his utopian recreation of a medieval society is represented by himself through the Akroyd shield and carved stags' heads and oak leaf wreaths.

On the north side was an extract from Book VI of Wordsworth's *Excursion*, emphasising the messages of the entire monument as Wordsworth's work refers to freedom, the sovereign, and the church, ornamental interest on churches as well as human charity and social love.[39]

The monument is indebted to Scott's Martyrs' Memorial in Oxford, a memorial with which both Akroyd and Barber would have been familiar. For Akroyd, it was plainly much more than an attractive finishing touch for the park. It carried the messages he wanted to make and was effectively his retirement speech, cast in stone, made as he left Parliament, in failing health and out of step with the Liberal Party. The Victoria Cross was 'less a homage to Victoria than to the British Constitution she headed.'[40]

In 1894, land for the second phase of Akroydon was auctioned. By then Edward Akroyd had been dead six years and those who continued the building of the community had none of his medievalising passion. The realisation of his utopian dream passed away with him.

BEDFORD PARK, CHISWICK, W. | Close to TURNHAM GREEN STA
Trains every few minutes.

THE HEALTHIEST PLACE IN THE WORLD | The Estate is built on gravelly Soil
the most approved Sanitary arran

(Annual Death Rate under 6 per Thousand).

About 500 Houses on the Estate, all in the picturesque Queen Anne style of Architecture.

A Garden and a Bath Room with Hot and Cold water to every house, whatever its s
A Kindergarten and good Cheap Day Schools on the Estate, and a School of Art.
Also Church, Club (for Ladies & Gentlemen), Stores, "The Tabard Inn," Tennis Court
Several houses now to let at rents varying from £30 to £130.

3.1 Bedford Park: 1882 advertisement. An early understanding of advertising skills is
demonstrated in this example of Victorian marketing. The image has been manipu-
lated to enhance aesthetic appeal: the foreground garden and the church are enlarged
to increase their attractiveness (*St Michael and All Angels' Church, Bedford Park*)

3

The Marketing Aesthetics of Bedford Park

Jonathan Carr and Bedford Park

Bedford Park was conceptually quite different from both Saltaire and Akroydon, being a speculative housing development by Jonathan Carr (1845-1915) in response to the then new phenomenon of what is now known as a 'market' for housing. The demand was from the growing middle class and the designs were to suit their tastes. Whereas the Yorkshire communities had been provided for working people by wealthy industrialists and built to their founder's specifications, Bedford Park was built to designs to suit the purchasers. For Jonathan Carr, it was a business opportunity but it also dangled the opportunity for him to live as lord of the manor. Carr understood the essentials of marketing a full half century before it was formally recognised as a discipline in Britain. It 'resulted in a unique, even utopian, community'.[1]

Carr was one of a large Battersea family with artistic interests and radical political leanings and was university educated. His brother, J Comyns Carr, art critic, writer and founder of the Grosvenor Gallery, became a publicist whose innovative designs in the new field of advertising were to prove critical in marketing the new community. He was able to capitalise on the enormously attractive site – a still-rural location but within 30 minutes of the City on the newly opened railway with a station at Turnham Green and at the convergence of existing main roads.

Jonathan Carr acquired his initial parcel of land in 1875. At the time, speculative builders were building terraces for those able to afford to buy their own home, of largely indistinguishable 'ill proportioned houses

CORNER PROS=
PECT OF ONE
OF THE NEW ROA=
DS ON THE BEDF=
ORD PARK ESTATE

3.2 E W Godwin's design for the first two houses, 1 and 2 The Avenue (*The Victorian Society*)

covered in gimcrack ornament, the fatal result of Ruskin's over-enthusiastic propaganda'.[2] Inspired by the Aesthetic Movement which developed from the 1870s and capitalising on the new interest in vernacular buildings, he identified his market as the aspirational middle class of modest means and planned Bedford Park to appeal to them. This was truly innovatory – a first attempt to build moderately priced yet attractive homes for the new middle classes,[3] people who, whilst not wealthy, had been educated to appreciate beauty in architecture and the decorative arts. They had been inspired by the Great Exhibition of 1851 and were acquiring a taste for art and interior decoration: they wanted some sort of ornamentation on their houses but disliked the heaviness and fussiness considered attractive in the preceding decades. Carr's intention was to charge rents for aesthetically pleasing houses that were comparable to those of typical, less attractive, Victorian estates.[4] The 'Queen Anne Revival' style of the houses of Bedford Park can be traced to Red House (1859), the home that Philip Webb designed for and with William Morris.

Beginning the community
Building began in 1875-76, with Carr's initial purchase of land. His first

architect was the 'arch aesthete'[5] E W Godwin (1833–86), whose architectural designs, as well as those for furniture and furnishings, were popular with the Aesthetic Movement. Carr had seen an example of Godwin's work – a simple brick and tile design – and liked its artistic quality. The design followed the Red House example in abandoning the subordination of internal function to external appearance so the house made the convenience of the inhabitants of paramount importance. A further attraction to Carr was that it was also cheap. Having identified the growing demand from the increasing middle class for affordable houses that had some aesthetic interest and a greater functionality than Gothic style houses permitted, Godwin's design seemed ideal.

Carr commissioned three designs from Godwin and in 1876 the first two houses were built – 1 and 2 The Avenue **(3.2)**. They were externally very simple in order to reduce building costs. Altogether, eighteen show houses were planned, including some modified by architects Coe and Robinson. Nonetheless, Godwin's association with the project was short: he was dissatisfied with the way builders handled his designs, annoyed by Carr's financial restrictions and by criticisms in the building press of his handling of interior space. Carr, though, was already formulating his plan for a new kind of estate to appeal to his new market: an informal layout, in which attractive houses would be built, retaining as many mature trees as possible to create an established appearance from the beginning – and he would make these houses available at cheap rents.[6]

Picturesque houses had previously been the prerogative of the rich since any deviation from the conventional, even in interior decoration, had been too expensive for the average householder. Carr decided that if sufficient numbers wanted interesting houses and artistic decoration it should be possible for his architects to produce varied results from permutations of a limited number of designs, allowing materials to be bought in large quantities. Thus the picturesque could be made affordable. This was the core of Carr's innovatory idea and the Queen Anne style lent itself well to his purpose. Furthermore, although the village was to be a speculative development, Carr planned to live there himself, so he invested more concern in the project than might otherwise have been the case.

The appointment of Richard Norman Shaw

Carr appointed Shaw, then at the peak of his career, as the estate architect and 'could hardly have made a better choice'.[7] It was Shaw who went on to determine the style of the buildings of Bedford Park, for which the main criterion was that the housing was to be visually pleasing. It was also Shaw

3.3 Richard Norman Shaw's elevation of asymmetrical semi-detached houses (*The Victorian Society*)

who chose the picturesque and newly fashionable Queen Anne Revival style and, since he also designed most of the public buildings, he became the architect most strongly associated with Bedford Park, whose 'unique character [was] bequeathed by Carr's inspiration and Shaw's genius'.[8]

Shaw's relationship with Carr was never more than a business relationship but Carr liked his style, sometimes having it adapted by other architects. The other architects who contributed to Bedford Park were all associated with Shaw and included his assistants, Edward John May (1853-1941) and Maurice B Adams (1849-1933), resident on the estate for many years and editor of *Building News*, through which position he was able to keep the estate's development in the public eye. Local architect William Wilson (1856-1928)[9] oversaw the implementation of Shaw's plans up to 1880.

Carr himself determined the layout with the assistance of Wilson while Shaw: 'provided a series of practical, picturesquely varied and inventive designs in the Queen Anne revival manner but exercised no supervision'.[10]

He provided six designs altogether which were interpreted in different ways by Wilson.

Variety from a few core design elements

The most prominent feature was the use of red bricks and tiles, rather than the then generally used London yellow stock brick, stucco and slate. As in other areas of art at the time, simplicity was an essential feature and, in the majority of houses, it was the design of the houses themselves rather than any added embellishment that created decorative effects. Distinctive design elements included steep roofs, tile-hanging, dormers, tall chimneys, bay windows, gables (often in the Flemish style associated with the Queen Anne Revival), balconies, front gardens surrounded by wooden fences and woodwork generally painted white. Different permutations of these features enhanced the picturesque effect. This was a dramatically different approach to building from that in Saltaire or Akroydon and enabled easy individualisation instead of the uniformity more general in the Yorkshire communities.

Shaw designed terraces, detached houses (for corner sites) and semi-detached houses, the latter of which were the most popular. A particularly simple but innovatory technique to add interest to these houses was to

3.4 The 'irregular charm' of the asymmetrical 16 and 18 Priory Avenue

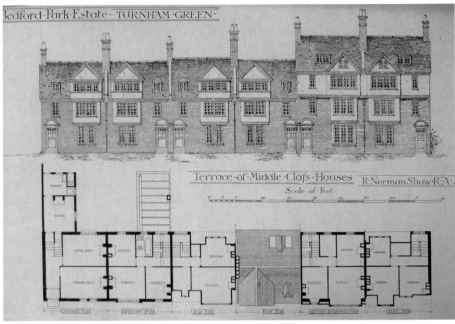

3.5 Shaw's elevation of an asymmetrical terrace (*The Victorian Society*)

3.6 Flemish-style gables at 28 The Avenue. This is one of the styles used on several houses on the estate

3.7 Alternative Flemish-style gables at 10 Queen Anne's Grove. The simple addition of paint to a standard design permitted greater individualisation of houses

employ a different design for each of the pair: 16 and 18 Priory Avenue, for instance, are examples where one of the pair has a gable while the other has a dormer **(3.3, 3.4)** so that 'from the outside they have the same irregular charm as the old English village Bedford Park was intended to recall'.[11] The asymmetry relieved the uniformity of three-bedroomed semi-detached styling. The idea appears elsewhere, including his terrace design for 24–34 Woodstock Road **(3.5)**. Another of Shaw's designs embellished pairs of houses with Queen Anne Flemish-style gables, which was a 'treatment quite foreign to the prevailing English village atmosphere'[12] but which contributed to the unique feel of the community **(3.6, 3.7)**.

3.8 Tile hanging, 20 Woodstock Road. Tile hanging was used in combination with other design devices on numerous houses on the estate and helped to distinguish houses from essentially similar properties nearby

3.9 A built-out chimney at 13 Blenheim Road. This was a popular design feature, recalling the country cottages that were the inspiration for the architectural style of the estate

Tile-hanging was used widely, sometimes simply filling a gable but often covering the entire upper storey of a house **(3.8)**. Tall, built-out cottage-style chimneys were frequent and varied in style **(3.9)**. Windows offered many opportunities for variety **(3.10)**. Small windows necessary for internal illumination were sometimes made a design feature, as were tall windows lighting staircases **(3.11)**. A repeated window style that gave the Bedford Park houses a distinctive appearance was the so-called 'Ipswich bay' which had an arched motif in the centre **(3.12)**.

Wood was cheaper than stone and easier to work. Andrew Saint notes the importance of this in the amount of integral wooden ornamentation: 'The details are of course adapted to the skills and materials available, so that balconies proliferate but stone carving is minimised.'[13] The balconies at first-floor level or above are of varying quality and styles but are all visually striking **(3.13)**. The one uniform feature was the almost ubiquitous use of white paint for external woodwork and it was this, particularly on fencing **(3.14)** and gate arches that achieved a visual unity in the village

3.10 A variety of windows achieved individuality on a detached house on the corner of Woodstock Road

3.11 Shaw's elevation showing a long window for illuminating the staircase (*The Victorian Society*)

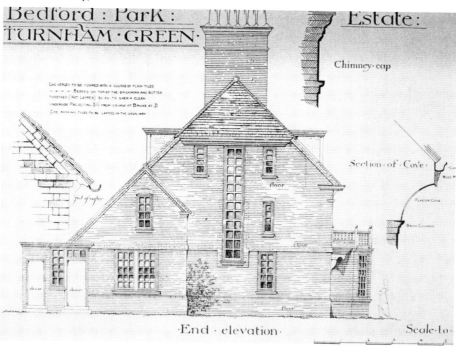

69

3.12 (above) Ipswich bays at 12 and 14 Woodstock Road. These were a popular and fashionable style of window on the estate

3.13 (below) First-floor balconies at 3 and 5 Woodstock Road. Constructed in wood and painted white, these were a low cost way of making the appearance of ordinary semi-detached houses very striking

3.14 White garden fences at 23–29 Priory Avenue. White paint on virtually all the front garden fences of the estate bound the individualised houses into a harmonious unity

3.15 A detached house on a corner site achieving a highly individual appearance from a mix of various standard decorative details (15 Priory Avenue)

3.16 The sunflower motif

3.17 (below) The 'sunflower houses': 20 and 22 The Avenue

3.18 Personalisation of a house by means of the owner's initials and the date of construction. The house was built for the artist Joseph Nash, at 36 The Avenue

while the mixing of design motifs achieved considerable individualisation **(3.15)**. Some styles were tried but not repeated for reasons of economy: the installation of large joists to support big windows, for instance, proved particularly uneconomical.

Decoration

Apart from integral design features, there was a very limited use of terracotta mouldings (which were popular with aesthetes) and other added devices for decoration. Shaw initially intended extensive use in terracotta of sunflowers **(3.16)**, one of the emblems of the Aesthetic Movement, but after use on his first two pairs of semi-detached houses (19 and 21 with 20 and 22 The Avenue), this was abandoned for reasons of cost. Also in these houses was an imaginative use of fenestration: 'Each differently sized window which Shaw used in the sunflower semidetached plan is perfectly matched to the space it illuminates',[14] but this also proved too costly and was not repeated **(3.17)**.

To overcome the problem of expense in the use of decorative mouldings, prospective home-owners were able to pay extra for embellishments of their

3.19 Terracotta moulding on the side of 1 Priory Gardens, dating the construction of a whole road.

choice such that 'Bedford Park is a textbook example of the capabilities of Queen Anne, because the people for whom the houses were designed were allowed to make requests about specifications ... [whilst] still retaining the architectural integrity of the area'.[15]

Some chose to identify their new home, as in Akroydon, with their initials and the date of construction. Shaw's house for the artist Joseph Nash at 36 The Avenue is an example **(3.18)**. Terracotta motifs appeared again on some of the later housing. Examples include a plaque on the side of 1 Priory Gardens which records the date of the building of the whole road **(3.19)** and a stylised flower on the wall of 4 The Orchard **(3.20)**.

3.20 Terracotta mouldings were used again on some of the later houses: a stylised flower on 4 The Orchard

3.21 Shaw's garden front elevation of Tower House, built for Jonathan Carr. This was the largest house on the estate, where Carr created for himself a lifestyle that enabled him to imagine that he was lord of the manor (*The Victorian Society*)

The public buildings and Tower House

It seems that Carr's original plan was not for a self-contained community but simply for a housing estate for the middle classes as the first mention of a projected church and club was not until 1877.[16] Shaw took personal responsibility for the public buildings – the most prestigious buildings of the development – including the church, club and inn. He also designed Jonathan Carr's own impressive house, which was an early commission. Centrally located in the estate and 'one of his best designs',[17] Tower House was built in 1878 **(3.21)**. It was surmounted by a balustrade and a cupola and surrounded by large gardens which were an attempt to recreate an old English type of garden.

The Club **(3.22)**, a true Queen Anne design by E J May but attributed to Shaw, opened in 1879 next to Tower House and was the first of the public buildings. The grounds of the Club merged into the garden of Tower House whose tennis courts came to be seen as part of the Club. The foundation stone for the Church of St Michael and All Angels was laid in 1879 and the building was consecrated in 1880. The 'muscularity' of mid-Victorian

3.22 The Bedford Park Club, attributed to Richard Norman Shaw but designed by his assistant, E J May

3.23 Shaw's elevation for the stores, the inn and two private houses between. This is a curious mixture of building styles and shows Shaw experimenting with a variety of design influences (*The Victorian Society*)

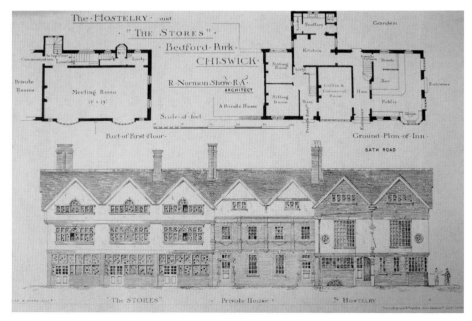

3.24 The Tabard Inn, which was decorated by artists of repute: the original inn-sign was designed by T M Rooke and interior tiles were designed by William De Morgan and Walter Crane

churches had fallen from favour and a more delicate style was sought. The style of the church is predominantly late Gothic with Queen Anne details such as the turret and the balustrade at clerestory level, a particularly novel embellishment, and the large porch to the main door.

The public buildings were completed by the Tabard Inn (1880) and the Bedford Park Stores on the Bath Road, constructed as one long building with two houses between the inn and the stores **(3.23, 3.24)**. This seems to have been another stylistic experiment: the gabled main structure of brick and rough cast surfaces is in seventeenth-century style with Queen Anne decorative aspects, such as the windows. It is 'fused into a single design by the original handling and sense of proportion characteristic of Shaw's best work.'[18]

Later buildings

Shaw ceased his association with Bedford Park around 1881. E J May, his assistant, became estate architect on Shaw's departure, living at 6 Queen Anne Gardens, which permitted closer supervision than previously,

3.25 E J May's shell door-hood was integral to the design of the front door (5 Priory Gardens)

resulting in a better quality of building than on earlier parts of estate. He and Maurice B Adams were responsible for most designs in the 1880s. May's most attractive innovation was in Priory Gardens, built in 1880, while still working for Shaw, where shell door-hoods were used as a distinctive but integral decorative feature **(3.25)**.

May and Adams were also responsible for several of the larger houses in Newton Grove and The Orchard. Adams' design for 12 and 14 Newton Grove **(3.26)** for the artist J C Dollman, displays the most ornate door hoods and gables on the estate and his Flemish design for 5 The Orchard produced the largest house after Tower House. Adams was also responsible for the design of the Chiswick School of Art **(3.27)**, destroyed during the 1939-45 war. It was the last of the public buildings to be erected and it opened in 1881. It was a 'picturesque though not entirely satisfactory composition'.[19] By now, building design was of critical importance to Bedford Park's inhabitants and Shaw was asked to make improvements. He raised the central gable and redesigned the porch, and the design then apparently met with approval. It was a particularly decorated building, very much in the fashionable Flemish style including not only gables but also Flemish window shutters.

3.26 (above) Maurice B Adams' design for artist J C Dollman at 12 and 14 Newton Grove with ornamented gables and door hoods (*The Victorian Society*)

3.27 (below) Adams' drawing of the Chiswick School of Art with gables and shutters in the fashionable Flemish style (*The Victorian Society*)

3.28 William Morris wall-paper in a reconstructed Aesthetic interior at 1 Priory Gardens

3.29 William De Morgan tiles in The Tabard

In all, 350 red brick houses were built in more than 30 styles. By combining a small number of design features, both variety and unity was achieved – in marketing terms, a novel achievement in product development. It was the variety that made Bedford Park so different from other suburbs. With a church, stores, club and tavern, the village became a complete community and while most of the developing suburbs were dull and monotonous, Bedford Park was aesthetically interesting.

The aesthetic community

More than an architectural experiment though, with the development of a variety of activities from the outset, Bedford Park attracted the target market of creative people in a social experiment that lent a further aesthetic dimension to this utopian development. That social life was artistically particularly rich and busy is evident from the letters of J B Yeates,[20] the father of the poet W B Yeates. The family was resident on the estate for about a year from 1879. In 1888 they returned and Bedford Park became the family home for the next fourteen years. With a debating society, plays, poetry readings and sporting activities, the estate was a very fashionable place to live in the 1880s. Social life was focused on the Club and the tennis courts in Carr's garden, which, unusually for the time, welcomed women on equal terms to men. The inhabitants themselves made it an aesthetic and free-thinking community: 'Art mattered in Bedford Park ... [it was] one of the shaping forces in the community'.[21]

In a remarkable example of early market segmentation, houses with north-facing studios were designed specifically for painters (such as Adams' house for J C Dollman, and Wilson's house at 7 Queen Anne Gardens, for painter T M Rooke, studio assistant to Edward Burne-Jones). 18 and 20 Queen Anne Gardens were designed with top-floor studios under a mansard roof, especially to attract painters. The estate became home to artists, architects, actors, playwrights, writers and publishers with one in five households supported at some time by art.[22] At one point among the resident artists was Lucien Pissarro, who lived briefly at 62 Bath Road. The estate itself was sufficiently exciting for his visiting father, Camille Pissarro (1830–1903), to paint some local scenes in 1897.

Interior decoration

Interior decoration of their homes was particularly important to this artistic community. Fashionable colour schemes comprised subdued colours, particularly dull greens, in reaction to the harsh and bright colours of the middle of the century. Wallpapers from the studio of William Morris,

3.30 The 'modest and familiar' interior of St Michael and All Angels' Church

who lived nearby in Hammersmith, were ubiquitous and furniture was comparatively lightweight in contrast to the heavy earlier Victorian style **(3.28)**. The public buildings mostly reflected the new fashions in interior decoration. The walls of The Tabard Inn were generously decorated with tiles by William De Morgan **(3.29)** and tiles by Walter Crane ornamented the fireplace.

It was, however, the interior of the church that was particularly innovatory. Unlike Saltaire and Akroydon, it was modest and familiar, with the comfortable pews painted in the same fashionable dull green that aesthetes were using in their homes **(3.30)**. Shaw's detailing translated the Arts and Crafts style into ecclesiastical embellishment that was delicate and quite different from previous church decoration. His lectern was simple and slim with restrained natural carving and Adams' font and wooden pulpit also exhibited a new delicacy **(3.31–3.33)**.

Andrew Saint has suggested that Shaw was making a joke at Carr's expense in the theatricality of the church interior:

> seven grand steps up to the chancel, where the action occurs, a 'proscenium' screen in three sections, and easeful benches down in the

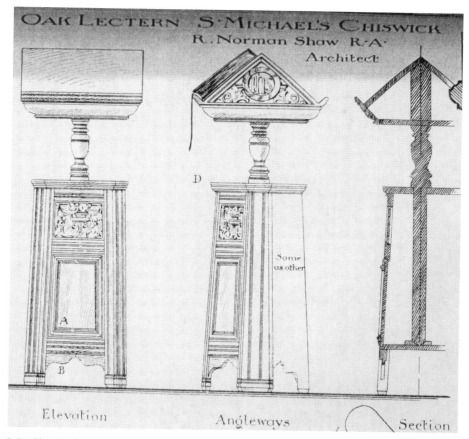

3.31 Shaw's drawings for the lectern, showing delicacy of design (*The Victorian Society*)

panelled nave, painted a sage green like all the woodwork … . In his pliant hands, St Michael's becomes the comfortable auditorium where independent, clear-thinking folk can watch the enactment of the Lord's Supper without loss of self-respect, without over-involvement, without incongruity with their other social activities. At a blow, the tension and vehemence of the mid-Victorian church is laid low. St Michael's symptomatizes a new attitude towards church-going.[23]

If so, it would have been a particularly audacious move on the part of a committed churchman – but Carr exasperated Shaw in taking his plans and putting them in the hands of builders without the competence to execute them properly. Furthermore, Shaw was probably never fully paid for his Bedford Park designs.[24]

3.32 Slim and delicate design made Adams' font strikingly modern

The demise

Unlike Akroydon and Saltaire where funds seemed unlimited, the development of Bedford Park was dogged by financial problems, necessitating the simplification of designs and economising on materials. By 1881 Carr was in financial difficulties and sold the land to the company Bedford Park Ltd, to continue the development of the estate, becoming Managing Director himself. By 1886, this had failed and westward expansion plans were abandoned with building on only about half the land purchased.[25] From 1887 the estate was broken up and the undeveloped land was sold piecemeal to a variety of builders who erected houses similar to Shaw's but lacking his flair. Heavily in debt Carr was obliged to sell Tower House in 1908.

The one noteworthy house of this later period was 14 South Parade, designed by C F A Voysey (1857-1941) and built in 1891 **(3.34)**.

Bedford Park was the natural place (being experimental in every way) for the house of no style to appear … a stylistic declaration of independence … an elegant, white, formal rectangular box, … In the fifteen years between the beginning of Bedford Park and the construction of this house it had become possible to conceive of a house without style imposed on it by an external conception of style, and it is significant that this new possibility was achieved in a community of houses which illustrated the variety of the most flexible of traditional styles.[26]

The house was described as 'white in Italian style'[27] but it was worlds away from Salt's Italianate village and Akroyd's 'Italian Trecento to Quattrocento' mansion. Its only decoration was delicate, thin gutter brackets. This house was so different from those built in Shaw's style – particularly in the deliberate return to stucco – that it caused much local protest.

3.33 Restrained carving in the design of Adams' pulpit distinguished it from the heavy ornamentation of just a few years before (*The Victorian Society*)

85

3.34 The provocative Italian style house by C F A Voysey at 14 South Parade, built in 1891

But Bedford Park's time was passing and the features that had made the community unique were appearing elsewhere. Jonathan Carr had been decades ahead of his time in understanding the principles of marketing: in the four essential elements of his 'marketing mix' he saw and exploited the benefits of Bedford Park's convenient location; he had an innate sense for product development and he had an extraordinarily modern understanding of promotional techniques. However, his pricing strategy was flawed: he failed to realise that his aesthetic houses could command higher prices than monotonous terraced houses and this error inevitably led to his downfall. It is surprising that he failed to apply one of the well understood axioms of other product markets: that for uniqueness or individualisation, customers are prepared to pay more than for a basic item. Furthermore, as any variation from a basic product has additional costs, even permutations of just a small number of design elements, Carr needed to cover his additional costs by charging higher prices for his houses. His financial difficulties were the result of his oversight and miscalculations – and he retired to impecunious obscurity, leaving an extraordinary and visionary dream to evaporate.

4

Conclusions

In drawing some conclusions from this study of the aesthetics of three communities all considered 'utopian' at some point in their development, it is clear that in Saltaire, Akroydon and Bedford Park decoration and appearance were of paramount importance. Furthermore, the results can be seen to have been the product of the beliefs, value systems, ideals and aspirations of their creators. In the case of Saltaire, those of the founder predominate but the influence of the architects is evident in numerous details. In Akroydon, the beliefs of the founder were of supreme importance while the architects and craftsmen involved used the opportunity of seemingly unlimited funding to create 'showcase' pieces of work. In Bedford Park, it was the architects rather than the founder who made the chief visual impact. Over the century and more since the building of these communities, it is evident, though, that it is the reputations of the architects of all three communities that have benefitted most. Despite statues erected by public subscription and still standing in Saltaire and Akroydon, and a plaque on the side of the Bedford Park church, Salt, Akroyd and Carr are less remembered than Henry Lockwood, George Gilbert Scott and Richard Norman Shaw whose reputations are at least partly dependent on their work in these model villages. All three communities remain today more or less intact and visually distinct from their surroundings but aesthetic tastes have changed and artwork has faded and they are mostly seen simply as quaint curiosities. Clearly 'Utopia' was no more than a visionary ideal. Their messages, no longer 'read' as they were in the nineteenth century, are lost or seem irrelevant.

In evaluating their architecture, as with all art forms, it is necessary to consider who created the work of art, for whom and with what purpose and whether it was successful in achieving that purpose. Both Titus Salt and Edward Akroyd, whatever their stated ideals, were seeking firstly to create in their utopias perpetual memorials to themselves. Nonetheless, the decoration in the architecture of their communities also sought to fulfil more subtle purposes. For both Salt and Akroyd, the architecture of their villages carried political messages. The grammar and vocabulary of these messages is no longer widely understood but in the nineteenth century, the language of the messages was clear. For Jonathan Carr, however, there were no messages and no subtle purpose – his utopia was a 'marketing response' to the needs and wants of the emerging middle class: he identified a market, designed a product to suit that market and promoted it to that market. It marked an abrupt change in the purposes to which architectural decoration was put. Gone was personal aggrandisement (although Carr revelled in life in Tower House) and the search for immortality through aesthetic devices and gone too was the wealth of paternalistic industrialists to lavish on grand pet projects. In their place was the search to genuinely improve through more modest projects, the lives of the thousands of new and aspiring urbanites. Bedford Park is therefore clearly an early example of what is now known as marketing.

In Saltaire, it was the public buildings that were the most impressive and their architecture, in its associations with grand nineteenth-century civic developments, was intended to denote progress through authoritarian though benign paternalism:

> The great public buildings which reflect the authority of the master – the factory, the church and the institute – dominate ... . The Gothic, reflecting the values of a traditional England, was reserved for the almshouses and the hospital, parts of the village not directly connected with the business of manufacturing. Everywhere else, a sort of '*quattrocento*' Italianate Renaissance style predominates. This ... invoked the aggressive individualism of early Italian Capitalism. The idea of progress was built into Saltaire.[1]

Titus Salt also used Saltaire to compensate for his inability to fully integrate into the lifestyle he had earned. At the age of 50, he chose to build the village rather than retire to the lifestyle of the landed gentry where he would have been out of place. The aesthetic aspects of the buildings emphasised what was most important to him: industry, religion and education. The aesthetics of his utopia were of the present and a unique attempt to set an example and ameliorate contemporary social problems by 'trying to marry the new technology and economic structure of the nineteenth century to the ordered authority of the pre-industrial world.'2

Salt also used the aesthetics of Saltaire to say what he was prevented from articulating by his lack of verbal skills: the architecture of Saltaire is solid and its decoration often unsubtle with frequently repeated messages. Salt was speaking at length in a way his character inhibited him from doing personally. Directness and frequency of message was appropriate when many of his workforce had only a limited education.

Italianate styling and its association with civic buildings proved attractive and Saltaire set the style for later mill buildings built for other industrialists. Yet the business declined and the mill was sold only a few years after Salt's death and with the sale the utopian dream faded.

Lockwood and Mawson earned their memorial in the village with the streets flanking the Institute named after them – the only streets named after people other than the monarch, her consort or members of the Salt family. After the early phases of the building of the village, they sought aesthetic ways to demonstrate their independence of Salt. They sometimes thumbed their noses at Salt – most notably in arguing aesthetic integrity in the additional storey in the almshouses and also in the jibe on an Institute keystone about the lack of a public house. Saltaire earned the architects a local reputation second to none and, in Lockwood's case, helped launch him nationally.

As a World Heritage Site, Saltaire's future seems assured. As a grade I listed building, the church remains architecturally important even if the reminders of the founder are now largely irrelevant. Salt's school became a secondary school when the local board school was opened and is now part of Shipley College – still in the forefront of local education as Salt wanted. His Institute never became a town hall and Saltaire was denied the autonomy its founder wanted. Tourists admire Salt's extraordinary buildings even if the purposes of their dramatic aesthetics are no longer appreciated. More importantly, though, Saltaire was an early experiment in town planning, where its aesthetic details no less than practical aspects continue to exert an influence.

Edward Akroyd's utopia was to be a blueprint for the future. Trying to base the future on the past can be seen in retrospect to be its fundamental flaw although this was precisely what was essential to Akroyd. His aesthetics tried to provide examples to follow in religion, social provision and liberal ideals but Akroydon did not become the social mix that Akroyd intended. His aesthetics were also part of his armoury in striving to become Halifax's first citizen, competing with – and finally losing out to – John Crossley. He yearned for a baronetcy so 'it is no wonder that he clung to the title of Colonel, even though it was honorific.'[3] His political attitude alienated him from those who might elevate him so he used the decoration of the structures in his utopia to convey idiosyncratic messages in defiance of those who would not listen. He squandered his fortune (his estate at death was worth only £1,234.00) in trying to create the kind of society he thought England needed, in trying to make others understand his ideas and also in seeking to establish himself in the position he thought he deserved in that society.

Akroyd's great gift to Halifax and his greatest memorial was All Souls' Church. The Church was described as a masterpiece and, though magnificent, might have been better but for his fanatical attempts to outshine Crossley. Scott himself, who was responsible for building hundreds of churches, while acknowledging it was: '…on the whole, my best church'[4], lamented:

> it labours under this disadvantage, that it was never meant to be so fine a work as it is, and consequently was not commenced on a sufficiently bold and comprehensive plan. Nothing could exceed the liberality and munificence of its founder, and I think he was well satisfied. I confess I hardly am so, as I know how much finer it would have been, had it been more developed as to size.[5]

As a redundant church and in the care of the Churches Conservation Trust, its importance as an architectural monument, particularly for its decoration, is now recognised. The lavishly appointed Akroyd mausoleum was demolished in 1968, the victim of irreparable vandalism. Akroyd's own home is a museum, sold to the local council before his death. The population of Akroydon was never the social hierarchy Akroyd sought, most probably because, despite his mortgage arrangements, the lowest paid working people could not afford the houses. The community around the Victoria Cross remains intact, opposite the museum and close to the church, and is part of the Boothtown area of Halifax. The name 'Akroydon' does not even appear on some maps and All Souls' Church is described as on Haley Hill rather than of Akroydon. Despite most of it remaining, it is as if Akroyd's community has been erased.

Bedford Park was, for its time, a futuristic development. In the 25 years between the beginning of Saltaire and the commencement of Bedford Park, the social fabric of the country had changed out of all recognition. By then the emergent middle class was both greater in numbers and better educated and there was no place for paternalism in their new world. The middle class had their own ideas, and the endowments of wealthy men, determined not only to leave a grand memorial to themselves but also to realise their personal notions of a better life, had no place.

The residents of Bedford Park were of limited means but they were beginning to enjoy discretionary spending. They were looking for a world to which they could relate, something smaller scale, simpler and more comfortable than the grand designs imposed by the benefactors of just a few years earlier. So, in the same year that Jonathan Carr began the building of Bedford Park with Godwin's simple villa, Salt's last building in Saltaire (the Congregational Sunday School) was opened – grandly Italianate and already aesthetically an anachronism. With the 1870 Education Act, the number of people demanding small, comfortable and attractive homes could only increase and the Queen Anne style of Bedford Park lent itself admirably to the individualisation that the new market demanded.

Bedford Park has been described retrospectively as the first garden city although it is Letchworth in the first years of the twentieth century that was actually built as such. In reality, it is clear that all three communities were steps in the development of the garden city. They gave lessons in the use of open space and the structures and institutions necessary to build a community but just as importantly, they demonstrated the importance of the aesthetic aspects of building. Saltaire showed how even small amounts of decoration on houses can make the monotonous interesting and increase self-respect, as well as the importance attached to a small private garden. Akroyden showed how beguiling the aesthetics of a mythical timeless heritage can be, while demonstrating for the first time (in the monogrammed houses) the value attached to individualisation. Bedford Park developed the concept of individualised private space by permutations of a few design features which offered the scope for inexpensive personalisation.

Gone was the paternalist and with him the symbolism incorporated into his designs. In its place was emerging the new concept of marketing: providing a new type of housing development in response to a demand. Not only Bedford Park, the utopian home for aesthetes, but also Saltaire and Akroydon set the pattern for the principal English contribution to late nineteenth-century architecture: the individualised detached or semi-detached house with its own garden. The aesthetic legacies of these would-be utopias are to be found in later projects such as Bournville, Port Sunlight, Letchworth, Hampstead and Welwyn and in twentieth century suburban housing developments worldwide. In this, the ideas of Salt, Akroyd and Carr were fundamental.

Notes

Chapter 1

1   Rev R Balgarnie, *Sir Titus Salt, Baronet: His Life and its Lessons*, originally published London, 1877, with commentary and additions by Barlo and D Shaw, Saltaire, 2003, 2

2   'Saltaire and its Founder', *The Graphic*, 13 January 1877, 44

3   Balgarnie (n 1), 65

4   Ibid, 88

5   Ibid, 142

6   Barlo and Shaw (n 1), 279

7   J Reynolds, *Saltaire*, Bradford, 1985, 21

8   R Clarke, in conversation with author, 18 August 2010

9   http://saltairedailyphoto.blogspot.com/2009/08/salt-family-coat-of-arms.html: accessed 21 August 2011

10 http://www.heraldry.ws/info/article05.html: accessed 21 August 2011

11 P Leach and N Pevsner, *The Buildings of England, Yorkshire West Riding, Leeds, Bradford and the North*, New Haven and London, 2009, 59

12 Ibid, 59

13 Ibid, 65

14 J Burgess, 'Lockwood and Mawson of Bradford and London', unpublished PhD thesis, De Montfort University, Leicester, 1998, 38

15 N Jackson, J Lintonbon, B Staples, *Saltaire: The Making of a Model Town*, Reading, 2010, 54

16 Balgarnie (n 1), 92

17 W Cudworth, *Round About Bradford: A Series of Sketches*, Bradford, 1876, 309

18 Balgarnie (n 1), 92

19 Leach and Pevsner (n 11), 680

20 Bradley, *Enlightened Entrepreneurs*, Oxford, 1987 and 2007, 41

21 J Burgess, 'Lockwood and Mawson of Bradford and London', unpublished PhD thesis, part 3, chronological gazetteer, no. 44, unpaginated

22 N Pevsner, *The Buildings of England, Yorkshire West Riding*, Harmondsworth, first published 1959, revised by Enid Radcliffe, 1979, 427

23 Balgarnie (n 1), 105

24 Burgess (n 21), no. 107

25 K Powell, *Pennine Mill Trail*, London, 1982, 14

26 Pevsner (n 22), 428

27 Ibid, 427

28 J Hole, *The Homes of the Working Classes*, London, 1866, 67

29 Jackson *et al* (n 15)

30 Jackson *et al* (n 15), 111

31 Ibid, 120

32 Burgess (n 21), no. 99

33 Leach and Pevsner (n 11), 58

34 Pevsner (n 22), 428

35 Reynolds (n 7), 19

36 Cudworth (n 17), 313

37 Burgess (n 21), 98

38 Ibid, no.105

39 A Holroyd, *Saltaire and its Founder*, Saltaire, 1871, 20

40 Ibid, 20

41 Reynolds (n 7), 13

42 Pevsner (n 22), 428

43 Cudworth (n 17), 313

44 Ibid, 228

45 Burgess (n 21), no. 122

46 Balgarnie (n 1), 106. In a footnote on p. 107 of the 2003 publication of Balgarnie's original biography, the editors, Barlo and Shaw, plainly somewhat sceptical of this story, refer to two further contemporary accounts that also assert that the lions at Saltaire were originally destined for Trafalgar Square

47 Holroyd, (n 39), 25

48 Anon, 'Some of the Stone Heads on Victoria Hall, said to represent Greek and Roman Deities', unsigned and unpublished MS, Shipley College Saltaire Archive, 1992

49 Holroyd (n 39) (n 39), 26

50 Reynolds (n 7), 13

51 Leach and Pevsner (n 11), 680

52 Burgess (n 21), no. 137

53 West Yorkshire Archives, Bradford, ref 72 D92/9/3

54 Balgarnie (n 1), 221

55 Holroyd, (n 39), 29

56 Ibid, 28

57 Burgess (n 21), no. 59

58 J Reynolds, *The Great Paternalist*, Bradford, 1983, 276

59 Royal Academy, *Eros to the Ritz: 100 Years of Street Architecture*, 2013

Chapter 2

1   A Whelan, 'The Victoria Cross in Akroydon: A Monument to the British Constitution', *Transactions of the Halifax Antiquarian Society*, new series, 12, 2004, 111

2   R Bretton, '*Colonel Edward Akroyd*', *Transactions of the Halifax Antiquarian Society*, 1948, 86

3   E Webster, '*Edward Akroyd*', *Transactions of the Halifax Antiquarian Society*, 1987, 30

4   Calderdale MBC, *Akroydon – its Past and Present*, Halifax, undated, 3

5   Bretton (n 2), 85

6   Ibid, 84

7   Ibid, 77

8   Ibid

9   Ibid, 95

10 D Cole, *The Work of Sir Gilbert Scott*, London, 1980, 141

11 Calderdale MBC (n 4), 5

12 J Wilkinson, 'Edward Akroyd Talk' typescript text, Bankfield Museum, Halifax, undated, 34

13 Bankfield Museum, Halifax, display material, 2005

14 Bretton (n 2), 82

15 P Howell, *All Souls' Church, Haley Hill, Halifax, West Yorkshire*, London, 2003, 2

16 Bretton (n 2), 82

17 Howell (n 15), 2

18 Ibid, 4

19 Whelan (n 1), 110

20 L Pearson, *Building the West Riding*, Otley, 1994, 134

21 Howell (n 15), 5

22 K Harrison, in conversation with author, 20 August 2010

23 Bretton (n 2), 86

24 E Akroyd, *On Improved Dwellings for the Working Class: A Plan for Building them in Connection with Benefit Building Societies*, London, 1862, 7 (http://www.calderdale.gov.uk/wtw/search/controlservlet?PageId=Detail&DocId=100923 accessed 1 February 2010)

25 Ibid, 7

26 Ibid, 8

27 Ibid, 9

28 Ibid, 8

29 Ibid, 12

30 Ibid, 12

31 Ibid, 12

32 Whelan (n 1), 113

33 N Pevsner, *The Buildings of England, Yorkshire West Riding*, Harmondsworth, first published 1959, revised by Enid Radcliffe, 1979, 240

34 Bretton (n 2), 92

35 Pevsner (n 33), 240

36 Whelan (n 1), 111

37 Ibid, 120

38 Ibid, 117

39 Ibid, 115

40 Ibid, 114

Chapter 3

1   M J Bolsterli, *The Early Community at Bedford Park: The Pursuit of "Corporate Happiness" in the First Garden Suburb*, London and Henley, 1977, 47

2   T A Greeves, 'London's First Garden Suburb, Bedford Park, Chiswick', *Country Life*, 7 December 1967, 1524

3   Bolsterli, (n 1), 9

4   T A Greeves, *Guide to Bedford Park*, Bedford Park, London, first published 1983, revised edition 2004, 6

5   Bolsterli (n 1), 49

6   Greeves (n 4), 1

7   Greeves (n 2), 1529

8   R Gradidge, *Bedford Park 1875-1975*, exhibition catalogue, Bedford Park, 1975, 4

9   T A Greeves, 'Bedford Park', *The Victorian*, November 1999, 25

10 Gradidge (n 8), 2

11 Greeves (n 4), 9

12 Ibid, 9

13 A Saint, *Richard Norman Shaw*, New Haven and London, 1976, 210

14 T A Greeves, 'A Brief Architectural History of Bedford Park', in M Glazebrook (ed), *Artists and Architects of Bedford Park, 1875-1900*, London, 1967, 54

15 Bolsterli (n 1), 12

16 T A Greeves, 'The Making of a

Notes

Community, Bedford Park, Chiswick',
Country Life, 14 December 1967, 1600

17 Ibid, 1600
18 Ibid, 1601
19 Ibid
20 J B Yeates, *Letters from Bedford Park*,
    Dublin, 1972
21 Bolsterli (n 1), 67
22 Gradidge (n 8), 3
23 Saint (n 13), 209-10
24 Ibid, 210
25 E Aslin, *The Aesthetic Movement: Prelude
    to Art Nouveau*, London, 1981, 49
26 Bolsterli (n 1), 56-7
27 Ibid, 57

Chapter 4

1 J Reynolds, 'Reflections on Saltaire' in
   J A Jowitt (ed), *Model Industrial
   Communities in Mid-Nineteenth Century
   Yorkshire*, Bradford, 1986, 48
2 J Reynolds, *Saltaire*, Bradford, 1985, 13
3 J Wilkinson, 'Edward Akroyd Talk',
   typescript text, Halifax, undated, 34
4 G G Scott, *Personal and Professional
   Recollections*, originally published 1879, new
   edition, Stamford, 1995, 176
5 Ibid

Bibliography

General

I Bradley, *Enlightened Entrepreneurs*, Oxford, 1987 and 2007
B Disraeli, *Sybil or the Two Nations*, London, 1881
D Linstrum, *West Yorkshire Architects and Architecture*, London, 1978
M Millar, *English Garden Cities: An Introduction*, Swindon, 2010
http://www.heraldry.ws/info/article05.html accessed 28 July 2011

Saltaire

Anon, 'Some of the Stone Heads on Victoria Hall, said to represent Greek and Roman Deities',
    unsigned and unpublished MS, Shipley College Saltaire Archive, 1992
W E Alderson, *Salt and Saltaire*, Shipley, 1986
Rev R Balgarnie, *Sir Titus Salt, Baronet: His Life and its Lessons*, originally published London,
    1877, with commentary and additions by Barlo and Shaw, Saltaire, 2003
J Burgess, 'Lockwood and Mawson of Bradford and London', unpublished PhD thesis, De
    Montfort University, Leicester, 1998
W Cudworth, *Round About Bradford: A Series of Sketches*, Bradford, 1876
J Greenhalf, *Salt and Silver: A Story of Hope*, Bradford, 1998
The Graphic, 13 January 1877
J Hole, *The Homes of the Working Classes*, London, 1866
A Holroyd, *Saltaire and its Founder, Sir Titus Salt, Bart*, Saltaire, 1871
N Jackson, J Lintonbon, B Staples, *Saltaire: The Making of a Model Town*, Reading, 2010
J A Jowitt (ed), *Model Industrial Communities in Mid-Nineteenth Century Yorkshire*, Bradford, 1986
P Leach and N Pevsner, *The Buildings of England, Yorkshire West Riding, Leeds, Bradford and the
    North*, New Haven and London, 2009
Morning Chronicle, publishing item from *Bradford Observer*, 7 October 1852, 'Mr Salt's Gigantic
    Factory'
L F Pearson, *Building the West Riding: A Guide to its Architecture and History*, Otley, 1994
N Pevsner, *The Buildings of England: Yorkshire West Riding*, Harmondsworth, 1959, revised by E
    Radcliffe, 1979
K Powell, *Pennine Mill Trail*, London, 1982
J Reynolds, *The Great Paternalist*, Bradford, 1983
J Reynolds, *Saltaire*, Bradford, 1985
West Yorkshire Archives, Bradford, 'Transverse section of the Congregational Sunday School,
    Victoria Road, Saltaire', ref 72 D92/9/3
http://saltairedailyphoto.blogspot.com/2009/08/salt-family-coat-of-arms.html accessed 21
    August 2011

Akroydon

E Akroyd, *On Improved Dwellings for the Working Class: A Plan for Building them in Connection with
    Benefit Building Societies,* London, 1862, 7 (http://www.calderdale.gov.uk/wtw/search/contr
    olservlet?PageId=Detail&DocId=10092 accessed 1 February 2010)
R Bretton, 'Colonel Edward Akroyd', *Transactions of the Halifax Antiquarian Society*, Halifax,
    1948, 61-96
Calderdale MBC, *Akroydon Heritage Trail*, Halifax, undated
Calderdale MBC, *Akroydon – its Past and Present*, Halifax, undated
Calderdale MBC, *From Weaver to Web*, Online Visual Archive of Calderdale History http://
    www.calderdale.gov.uk/wtw/search/controlservlet?PageId=Detail&DocId=100923
    accessed 1 February 2010

Bibliography

D Cole, *The Work of Sir Gilbert Scott*, London, 1980

P Howell, *All Souls' Church, Haley Hill, Halifax, West Yorkshire*, London, 2003

G G Scott, *Personal and Professional Recollections*, London, 1879, new edition, G Stamp (ed), Stamford, 1995

E Webster, 'Edward Akroyd', *Transactions of the Halifax Antiquarian Society*, Halifax, 1987, 19-45

A Whelan, 'The Victoria Cross in Akroydon: A Monument to the British Constitution', *Transactions of the Halifax Antiquarian Society*, new series, 12, 2004, 104-21

J Wilkinson, typescript text of 'Edward Akroyd Talk', Bankfield Museum, Halifax, undated and unpublished

Bedford Park

Anon, *Artists and Architecture of Bedford Park, 1875-1900*, catalogue of an exhibition held at St Michael and All Angels Church, Bedford Park during Bedford Park Festival Week, 10-18 June 1967

E Aslin, *The Aesthetic Movement: Prelude to Art Nouveau*, London, 1981

M J Bolsterli, *The Early Community at Bedford Park: The Pursuit of 'Corporate Happiness' in the First Garden Suburb*, London and Henley, 1977

R Gradidge and G Horner, *Bedford Park, The First Garden Suburb*, Bedford Park, 1975

T A Greeves, 'Bedford Park', *The Victorian*, November 1999, 25

T A Greeves, 'A Brief Architectural History of Bedford Park', in M Glazebrook (ed), *Artists and Architects of Bedford Park, 1875-1900*, London, 1967

T A Greeves, *Guide to Bedford Park*, Bedford Park, 1983, revised 2004

T A Greeves, 'London's First Garden Suburb: Bedford Park, Chiswick', *Country Life*, 7 December 1967, 1524-9

T A Greeves, 'London's First Garden Suburb', *Country Life*, 27 November 1975, 1446-8

T A Greeves, 'The Making of a Community: Bedford Park, Chiswick', *Country Life*, 14 December 1967, 1601-2

A Saint, *Richard Norman Shaw*, New Haven and London, 1976, revised edition 2010

J B Yeates, *Letters from Bedford Park*, Dublin, 1972

Sources of images

All images are from the author's collection except for the following:

1.15, 1.16, 1.20, 1.26, courtesy of Shipley College Saltaire Archive, which provided the photographic copies. The photographs were contemporary to the building of Saltaire but are undated.

2.1 Akroydon, All Souls' Church, courtesy of Geoff Brandwood.

3.1 Bedford Park, 1882 advertisement, courtesy of St Michael and All Angels' Church, Bedford Park.

3.2, 3.3, 3.5, 3.11, 3.21, 3.23, 3.26, 3.27, 3.31, courtesy of The Victorian Society, which granted access to its collection of lithographs by Maurice B Adams dating from between 1873 and his retirement in 1923, many of which are the copies of the work of other architects and which were originally published in *Building News*.